BUILDING THE NUTSHELL PRAM

by Maynard Bray, photos by Anne Bray

INTRODUCTION

These are the instructions for building the NUTSHELL pram—in our opinion, one of the best tenders ever designed. She's good to look at, easy to build, and does her job far, far better than most boats of her length. Joel White created the design and personally built the first two boats; this is what he has to say about the NUTSHELL:

"Little boats are fun to develop, but not so easy. The design constraints are so strong, and the requirements are so firm, that plans for a small boat can be a real challenge. This little packet grew out of a discussion with Jon Wilson and Maynard Bray last winter about why so many designs for plywood boats are complicated, unattractive, and unsuccessful. It was felt that there are lots of people who could and would build themselves a plywood boat if there were more good choices.

"One of the requirements was that it must be constructed from 8' panels, so the pram is 7'7" overall. An earlier plywood pulling boat I built with glued laps proved such a success that the same construction is used here. It produces a strong, light, easily constructed hull, and one that is so uncluttered inside that cleaning and painting it become quick and easy. It also makes for a boat that can be built with a minimum of pieces—a plus for the kit–boat purchaser. The rowing model of the NUTSHELL has only 27 wooden parts—not counting the oars.

"What we were after was a small pram that rowed and towed well, could carry a big load, and one that would really be fun to sail for both adults and children. The enthusiasm generated by the two prototypes has been contagious, and it seems as though these basic requirements have been met to a large degree. I am astounded at how easily she rows, and at her stiffness and speed under sail. But her best performance seems to be in generating fun—people come back from a trial row or sail with a grin and a request to try her again.

"After the success of the 7'7" model, we felt that a larger version, to be built with 10' plywood panels, would be desirable, so I designed the 9'6" NUTSHELL as a big sister having the same construction, appearance, and other attributes. Both have proven to be most useful little boats."

Even though the primary purpose of these instructions is to help you put the 7'7" kit together, they can also be used, along with the appropriate drawings, for guidance in building both the 7'7" and 9'6" NUTSHELLs from scratch. Keep in mind, however, that in some instances the 9'6" model's dimensions are different from those specified herein, and that *in those instances the drawings should prevail.*

GETTING STARTED

All of us involved with the design and kit have tried to make the NUTSHELL easy for you to build, even if it's your first boatbuilding project. But please, before you begin putting your kit together, study the plans and the detailed instructions so you'll be familiar with the terminology and the building process. Generally, the sequence of steps goes like this:

A) Build the station molds and the building jig. (Wood for these is common lumber and plywood and isn't included in the kit.)

B) Set the jig on legs or sawhorses at a convenient working height, leveled both ways.

C) Set the molds, the two transoms, and the 'midship frame on the jig so they are centered, plumbed (except for the transoms), and otherwise in the correct location.

D) Install the bottom panel, then the garboard planks, then the middle planks, and finally the sheerstrakes to complete the planking process.

E) Break the boat loose from its building jig and temporary molds, and turn it right-side up for completion of its interior.

F) Install the seats, quarter knees, guardrails, daggerboard trunk (if you're building the sailing model), oarlock sockets, etc.

G) Invert the hull once again, and install the outer keel and the metal chafing strip that protects it.

H) Prepare the surfaces and paint your new pride and joy.

The above steps are explained in more detail in the following pages, and you'll find that there are photographs there to guide you as well. We've had a boat built specifically to prove the adequacy of our plans, instructions, and the pieces that make up the kit, so you should have an easy and, we hope, enjoyable time building the NUTSHELL. But if for any reason you get into trouble partway along, or need some help or advice, drop us a line and we'll get back to you. Our address for pram correspondence is: NUTSHELL, c/o WoodenBoat, P.O. Box 78, Brooklin, Maine 04616.

If, after studying these instructions, you feel the need for some additional guidance, consider purchasing WoodenBoat's 90-minute video, "How to Build the NUTSHELL pram." If you're a beginning boatbuilder and place any value on your labor, its cost ($59.95) will be well worth your savings in time. The WoodenBoat School also offers a one-week course in building the NUTSHELL pram. For a copy of the school's brochure, write: WoodenBoat School, P.O. Box 78, Brooklin, Maine 04616. To order the video, write: WoodenBoat Catalog (same address).

TOOLS

Now let's talk about what tools you'll need. The following is a *minimum* list, and most items are found in the average home workshop:

Claw hammer
Block plane
Smoothing plane
Spokeshave
Butt chisel, about 3/4"
Crosscut handsaw, fairly fine

Hacksaw
Tape or ruler
Framing square
Tri-square
Sliding bevel square
Spirit level
Set of twist drills in sizes to 1/4"
Countersink
Eggbeater hand drill (or small electric drill) with 1/4" or 3/8" chuck
C-clamps, about a half dozen 4" to 6"
Sharpening stone for edge tools
Manual screwdriver—the type of your choice as long as its bit fits the
    screw slots
Pencil
Wood rasp
Mill file (for metal)
Putty knife
Scraper
Center punch

Building time can be shortened somewhat if you have the use of the following *additional* tools. These are somewhat expensive, however, and unless you have use for them after the pram is finished (we hope, of course, that you'll go on building more boats), you may want to dispense with them and do your building with the more common hand tools (in the minimum list above):

Electric drill with 1/4" or 3/8" chuck
Electric screwdriver (or a screwdriver bit in a variable-speed electric
    drill)*
Drywall screwdriver (or a drywall bit for use with a variable-speed
    electric drill)**
Portable electric jointer plane
Bench grinder (for sharpening edge tools)
Sabersaw
Combination taper drill/countersink for the screw sizes used

Whatever tools you use, it's vitally important that you keep them sharp—always. Planes and chisels, particularly, dull quickly on the plywood edges where they have to cut through glue as well as wood. This means you'll have to sharpen up often, but it's really worth the time it takes; the tools push more easily and the results are more accurate.

*Driving screws with a power screwdriver is a one–handed operation and frees up the other hand to hold whatever piece you're fastening. Thus, the time-consuming process of clamping is, in many instances, eliminated. But, by taking more time and using clamps, equal results can be obtained with a hand screwdriver or a screwdriver bit in a bit brace.

**Drywall screws make wonderfully convenient temporary fastenings. They are driven (and later backed out) one-handed with a powerdriver made especially for the purpose. (A variable-speed electric drill with a special drywall bit can also be used, although you have to be more careful since it doesn't have an auto-stop.) Drywall screws can be reused a couple of times, and later on you'll find many uses for this type of fastening, besides in building the pram.

PLYWOOD

Your NUTSHELL pram kit comes with high-grade mahogany plywood rather than the more usual commercial grades of Douglas-fir. We're convinced the extra expense is well worth it, however, for this application. Fir plywood has too few plies, and is not dense enough for the glued-lap construction employed in the NUTSHELL. So, please, stick with only the premium-grade African mahogany marine plywood provided in your kit. This is a quality boatbuilding material and will ensure that your NUTSHELL will last a long time. If you spoil a piece, you can order a replacement from us.

EPOXY GLUE

There are a number of epoxies on the market and, used properly, most of them will work in sticking your pram together. We've found that, generally speaking, the thicker stuff (thick like honey) works best on this job, as it doesn't soak into the porous beveled edges of the plywood. But, with care, you can get satisfactory results with thinner epoxy. With the thin stuff, you'll probably have to prime the surfaces with a coat of it before applying the final bonding coat. Just make certain, no matter what kind of epoxy you use, that there is an ample coating on both contact surfaces, one that shows wet and isn't going to disappear into the wood grain before you bring the pieces together for curing. And always follow the manufacturer's instructions for mixing, curing temperature, etc. If you're working in cold weather, be sure to use an epoxy that is formulated for this situation.

As a safeguard, we recommend applying a thin coating of epoxy over all exposed edges of plywood. This keeps out the moisture and greatly reduces the risk of subsequent rot or delamination.

You'll find that we call for a number of joints to be fastened by screws as well as epoxy. Do your fitting and drilling first, then clean up the contact surfaces and apply the epoxy. That way, you won't have the chips from the drilling operation caught in the glue line and preventing wood-to-wood contact.

KIT CONTENTS

When you've studied the drawings and have become familiar with the names of the pieces making up your kit, check each piece against the illustrated parts list on the following page to make sure you received everything you'll need. There are so few pieces, we didn't number the pieces themselves, but used their names in both our instructions and plans. We think you'll come to a better understanding if you call a garboard a garboard, for instance, instead of Piece 7.

THE DETAILED INSTRUCTIONS

If your kit is complete, if you've read the instructions, collected your tools, and brought your planes, chisels, etc., to a razor-sharp edge, it's time to begin setting up your NUTSHELL pram. Turn the page, and we'll show you how.

PARTS LIST

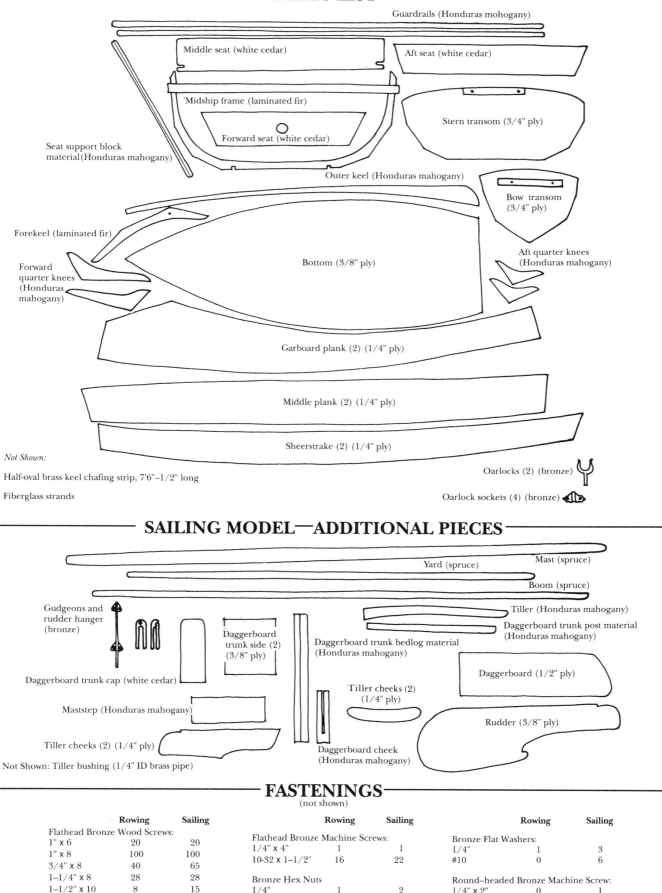

Guardrails (Honduras mohogany)

Middle seat (white cedar)

Aft seat (white cedar)

'Midship frame (laminated fir)

Stern transom (3/4" ply)

Forward seat (white cedar)

Seat support block material(Honduras mahogany)

Outer keel (Honduras mahogany)

Bow transom (3/4" ply)

Forekeel (laminated fir)

Forward quarter knees (Honduras mahogany)

Bottom (3/8" ply)

Aft quarter knees (Honduras mahogany)

Garboard plank (2) (1/4" ply)

Middle plank (2) (1/4" ply)

Sheerstrake (2) (1/4" ply)

Not Shown:

Half-oval brass keel chafing strip, 7'6"–1/2" long

Fiberglass strands

Oarlocks (2) (bronze)

Oarlock sockets (4) (bronze)

SAILING MODEL—ADDITIONAL PIECES

Yard (spruce)

Mast (spruce)

Boom (spruce)

Gudgeons and rudder hanger (bronze)

Daggerboard trunk side (2) (3/8" ply)

Daggerboard trunk bedlog material (Honduras mahogany)

Tiller (Honduras mahogany)

Daggerboard trunk post material (Honduras mahogany)

Daggerboard (1/2" ply)

Daggerboard trunk cap (white cedar)

Tiller cheeks (2) (1/4" ply)

Maststep (Honduras mahogany)

Rudder (3/8" ply)

Tiller cheeks (2) (1/4" ply)

Daggerboard cheek (Honduras mahogany)

Not Shown: Tiller bushing (1/4" ID brass pipe)

FASTENINGS
(not shown)

	Rowing	Sailing		Rowing	Sailing		Rowing	Sailing
Flathead Bronze Wood Screws:			Flathead Bronze Machine Screws:			Bronze Flat Washers:		
1" x 6	20	20	1/4" x 4"	1	1	1/4"	1	3
1" x 8	100	100	10-32 x 1-1/2"	16	22	#10	0	6
3/4" x 8	40	65						
1-1/4" x 8	28	28	Bronze Hex Nuts			Round–headed Bronze Machine Screw:		
1-1/2" x 10	8	15	1/4"	1	2	1/4" x 2"	0	1
2 x 14	12	12	10–32	16	22			

5

BUILDING THE MOLDS & JIG

The following instructions are for those who are building from a kit. If you're working from a set of plans only, see page 32 for additional information.

1 The building jig consists of a kind of ladder frame, made up from 2 x 4s and scrap pieces of 1" lumber. Its dimensions are clearly shown on the construction drawing, and this photo shows what it should generally look like when finished. Make sure the 2 x 4 rails are square with the cross spall, and that the jig is diagonally braced (notice the triangular piece of plywood on its underside in the photo below) to hold it that way.

2 When you've checked and rechecked that the jig is according to plan—particularly the 1 x 2" crosspieces that establish the mold and frame locations—nail the jig to sawhorses that are themselves nailed to the floor. But first, before nailing, shim the jig until it is exactly level, both fore-and-aft and athwartships. Then snap a chalkline down its center, as shown. (*Note:* Drywall screws can be used in place of nails in assembling and mounting the building jig.)

3 Two temporary molds will be needed to give the pram its shape for the planking operation. There are full-sized patterns included, and you can use 1/2" or 3/4" plywood for the molds themselves. (Material for molds and for the building jig is available "off the shelf" at any lumberyard; thus it has not been included with the kit.) To build the molds, simply lay each paper pattern on the plywood and prick through its outline with a pushpin, then connect the "dots" with a pencil line; alternatively, you can cut out the patterns and trace around them—one side at a time—as is being done here. Don't forget to transfer the mold's vertical centerline from the pattern to the wood. Saw to the marked outline of each mold.

SETTING UP

4 Fasten a 1 x 2" nailing cleat across the long edge of each mold as shown on the drawing. (One of these nailing cleats shows in this photo.) Each mold should then be centered, plumbed, fastened, and braced in its specified position on the jig.

5 The laminated 'midship frame comes next, and—as with the mold—it must be located and aligned with great care; it should be centered athwartships, set at the correct height (the cross spall that comes fastened to the frame should do this automatically, but it's a good idea to check the height measurement, anyway), and squared with the boat's fore-and-aft centerline. The frame can be plumbed and held that way later on, when the bottom panel is installed. This photo, and most of the subsequent ones, are of another setup—one in which the molds were built up of common lumber rather than plywood.

6 Now for the transom. On its inside face (the biggest one), you'll notice a temporary positioning cleat. This cleat, when brought up under the jig's aft crosspiece as shown in the plan, assures that the transom is at the correct height. Now you can set the transom in place against the uprights (raked 11° as shown), center it athwartships, and push it up until the temporary cleat contacts the jig's crosspiece. Check that the transom is level, and hold it temporarily with a couple of C-clamps while...

7 ...you drill for the four temporary screws that will hold it there.

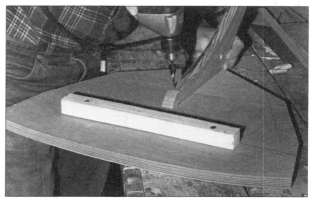

8 Draw two guidelines parallel to and 3/8" away from the marked centerline on the inner face of the bow transom. These are for locating the 3/4"-thick forekeel. Fasten the forekeel with three 1–1/4" #8 flathead bronze screws—one from the inside at the top of the fore keel as shown, and two from the outside (these show in the next photo). Always do the drilling before you spread the epoxy.

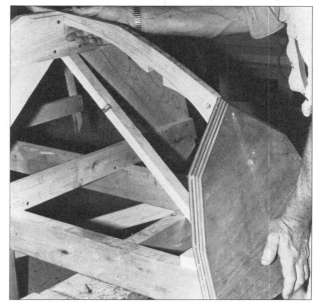

9 Here is the bow transom/forekeel assembly being positioned on the building jig. Note the two externally driven screws (called for in Step 8 above), and the 1/2" hole in the fore keel into which the boat's painter will later be spliced. The #1 station marks on the fore keel should align with the forward face of the #1 mold. (The notch in the fore keel shown in this photo can be ignored.)

10 The bow transom will almost align itself when you raise it so that the transom-mounted alignment cleat contacts the jig's crosspiece. The transom assembly should be centered athwartships, and it's a good idea to check that the unit is level (as is being done here) and that its height is correct. When it's all as it should be, the transom can be temporarily screwed to the jig.

PLANKING THE HULL

11 When you've checked and double-checked the alignment of everything—and it pays to be fussy about it—you can begin planking, with the bottom panel first. The reference lines marked on it go on the inside face. The bottom's fore-and-aft centerline should match up with the centerline markings on the transoms, molds, and frame. Similarly, the transverse markings on the bottom panel should correspond to the station lines: the forward face of the forward mold, the aft face of the laminated frame, and the aft face of the aft mold.

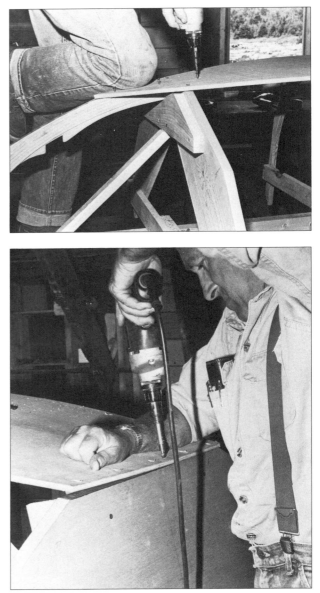

12 & 13 When you are satisfied that the bottom panel will fit all the reference lines and fit the boat as well, you can fasten it into place on the molds with drywall screws or other temporary fastenings, then drill for the permanent 1–1/4" #8 screws into the fore keel, transoms, and 'midship frame. When all the screw holes have been drilled (don't forget the countersinking), remove the bottom panel, clean the faying surfaces of shavings, and spread the epoxy. The screws can then be driven and will hold things together until the epoxy dries (the screws also back up the epoxy for the life of the boat).

14 Beveling the bottom panel comes next, and the object here is to plane a bevel that is fair along its entire length, yet matches the line of the molds, transom, and frame. *A temporary batten, similar to the one shown in Step 36, should be used to guide the beveling.* A fairly heavy plane, kept sharp and set coarse, works best in roughing out the bevel; a spokeshave works well, too.

15 Using the bottom corner of the plane as a straightedge is a convenient way of checking the bevel.

16 Finish the beveling with a smaller, more easily controlled plane—sharp and set fine. Make sure the beveled edges are fair curves without bumps or flat spots.

17 Then mark a centerline on the forekeel, and plane a bevel on both its corners—two opposing bevels that meet at the centerline. This operation has proven to be troublesome, and over-beveling is common among first-time builders. Take your time, and *use the batten-and-stick method shown in Step 36 if you have doubts about the proper beveling angle.* When complete, your bevels here on this fore keel and those on the edges of the bottom panel, 'midship frame, and the bow and stern transoms should yield a fair landing surface for the garboard planks—allowing them to rest against all the contact surfaces and, with epoxy, to produce a watertight seal. The ultimate test of the bevel comes in the next step when you dry-fit the garboards.

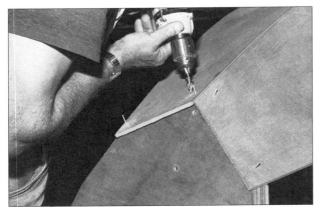

18 Position each garboard by aligning its reference mark with the 'midship frame and bringing its top (with the boat right-side up) edge to meet the knuckles of the molds, frame, and transoms. (If the alignment isn't precise at all five knuckles and you don't want to reshape the garboard's edge in pursuit of perfection, let the edge meet the knuckles where it will, and fall short of them where it has to; don't let the garboard overlap a knuckle, or you'll have problems in fitting the next plank.) Check to make sure the garboard overlaps the bottom panel and the transoms a little. The garboards should be planed as necessary to meet on the forekeel's centerline, and those edges should be left square to form a V-shaped seam that later will be filled with epoxy. As shown here, the garboards are temporarily held in place (by small nails driven in partway at each corner) while screw holes are being drilled. Work carefully as you drill the holes; because of the extreme bevel, it's easy to get them in the wrong place. As with all pieces that are to be both epoxied and screwed, the fitting and drilling should come first—before any epoxy is spread.

19 Epoxy may now be spread on the beveled edge of the bottom panel, and where the new garboard will lie on the 'midship frame, the fore keel, and the bow and stern transoms. A small piece of plastic or waxed paper over the edge of the molds will keep the epoxy away from them (and thus prevent your boat from sticking to its building jig).

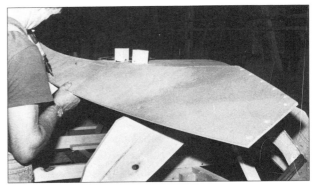

20 Here's the first garboard being installed. You've already drilled for the 1" #8 screws, so it's simply a process of lining up the holes and driving the screws.

21 The first garboard is now screwed to the fore keel. Be sure to clean up the excess epoxy before it hardens. (Masking tape and newspaper will keep epoxy from spreading beyond where you want it, but be sure to pull it off right after the pieces are clamped and fastened.)

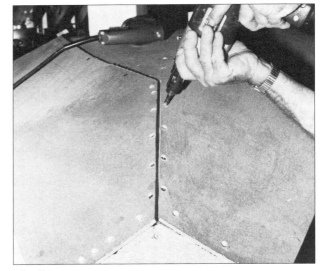

22 The second garboard goes on just like the first one. You'll have to slightly stagger the screws along the fore keel so you don't hit the ones already there.

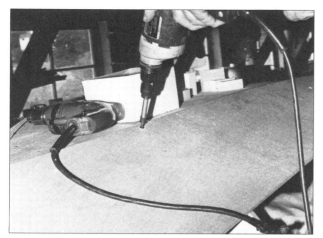

23 The beveled lap between the bottom panel and the garboards is held together with epoxy alone, as are the other plank laps. However, these laps must be squeezed together while the epoxy cures in order to form a strong watertight seal without voids. Although various ways of temporarily clamping the laps can and have been devised, we recommend the use of drywall screws.

24 We've found that there are two ways in which drywall screws can be used: You can pre-drill the laps and drive the screws through these holes and into softwood blocks (3/4 x 1 x 2–1/2") as shown in the photo, or you can simply drive the screws into the undrilled laps without the blocking. If you choose the latter method, however, be sure the screws are oriented to engage both layers so that the lap draws together as the screws tighten.

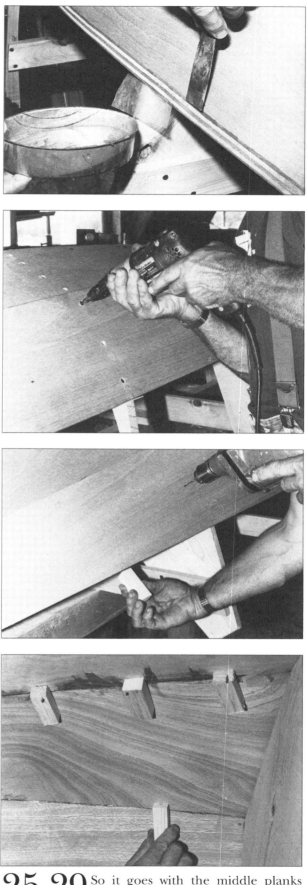

25-29 So it goes with the middle planks and with the sheerstrakes, using basically the same procedure as for the garboards:

(a) bevel to provide a fair and tight fit for the next plank; (b) dry fit the plank so that its lower edge comes even with the knuckles of the frame, molds, and transoms, and overlaps the adjoining plank fully*, (c) drill for its fastenings; (d) clean off the contact surfaces and spread them with epoxy; (e) fasten on the plank with 1" #8 screws driven into the holes you have pre-drilled into the frame and the transoms; (f) clamp the lap between the planks while the epoxy dries, using drywall screws or another method of your own choosing; (g) clean off the excess epoxy before it sets up.

*As noted in Step 38, the planks provided have been cut to slightly overlap the previous plank's beveled edge (between 1/8 and 1/4" is the usual amount). This is intentional and desirable, as it creates a V-shaped channel into which epoxy filler can be spread, thus increasing the gluing surface of the laps and adding to the boat's overall strength.

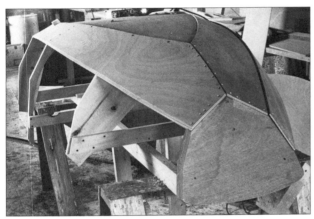

30 This is what your pram should look like when she is about half planked. The overlapping edge of the garboard has yet to be trimmed off flush with the bottom. The last plank will, of course, be the sheerstrake. Its edge should come to the sheerlines marked on the transoms and the 'midship frame.

31 Epoxy is applied to fill the centerline seam flush.

32 As you finish hanging each plank, it can be trimmed flush with the transom at the bow...

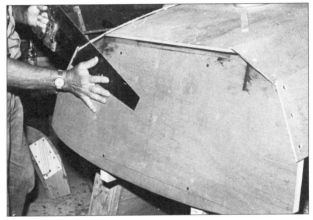

33 ...and at the stern.

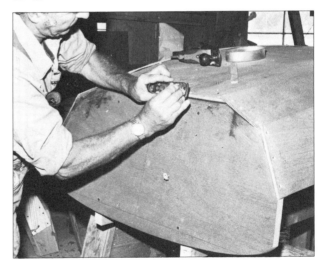

34 Planing, after sawing, brings the planks to their finished endings.

35 The garboards can be dressed down now, or you can wait until all the planking is complete. Use a hand plane or a spokeshave throughout, or do the rough cutting with a power plane (shown here) or a disc sander. The finished edges should be worked down until they are flush and fair with the bottom panel. Be sure the epoxy is fully cured, and don't forget to remove the temporary drywall screws before you begin. After planing is complete, coat the raw, beveled edge with epoxy resin to seal it.

36 It is easy to get carried away and cut too deeply when beveling the plank laps. Go slowly until you develop the knack, and check the accuracy of your bevel between control points by the method shown. This involves nailing a stiff, temporary batten (3/4 x 1" is about right) around the boat where the next plank's edge will lie, and holding a short straightedge at various points as shown, with its end against the inside of the batten. Your objective should be to have the bevel fair along its length, without humps or hollows, and always parallel to the straightedge. (This lap has been roughed out, and therefore looks wavy; it will be planed fair before the sheerstrake is installed.)

37 The bevel can be checked directly, of course, at the control points—that is, at the transoms, frame, and station molds. The plans show what the completed laps should look like; refer to them when in doubt.

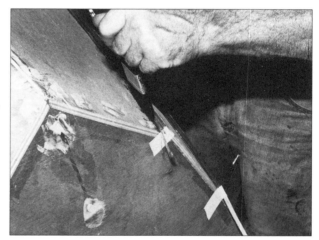

38 As mentioned earlier, the middle planks and the sheerstrakes have been cut to give a slight overhang at their laps on the outside of the boat. For extra strength, we recommend filling those overlaps with a couple of strands of fiberglass (provided), and embedding them in epoxy resin (the same resin you've been using on the rest of the boat). Masking tape helps avoid run-off and overspread. This is a good time, before turning the boat over, to fill all the screw holes and other gaps and holes with the filler of your choice. Polyester autobody putty (Bondo) works well; so does a mixture of epoxy and microballoons. After the filler has hardened, cut off the excess and sand it smooth.

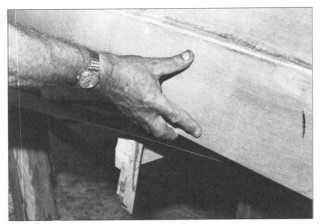

39 The time has come, finally, to cut the pram loose from its building jig and turn it right-side up for finishing. Start by sawing off the laminated frame between the sheerstrake and cross spall. Then back out any temporary fastenings that were driven into the building jig, such as those through the transoms and molds and transom positioning cleats, and you can lift the boat free and turn it over.

40 Now trim off the frame top as shown on the drawing, using saw, plane, and sandpaper.

THE KNEES

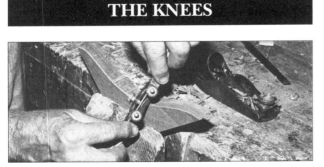

41 The four quarter knees come next. Begin by rounding their inboard corners and sanding their exposed surfaces smooth.

42 Scrape away any excess epoxy from the boat's aft corners providing a smooth seating surface for the quarter knees. Draw a line across the transom's inner face from sheer to sheer using a straightedge, measure up from this line to give each knee the same upward tilt, then bevel each knee's faying surfaces for a snug fit against the sheerstrake and the transom. When fitting is complete, mark each knee's outline on the transom.

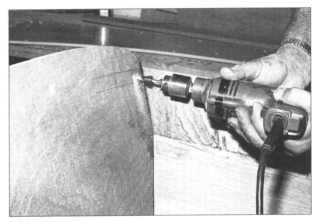

43 These marked lines are the guides between which you should drill two pilot holes out through the transom (to be used as locators later, when you drill from the outside for the screws themselves).

44 Now, for each knee, drill from the outside—at the proper angle (remember, the knee tilts upwards)—for three 1" #8 screws through the sheerstrake and two 1-1/2" #10 screws through the transom.

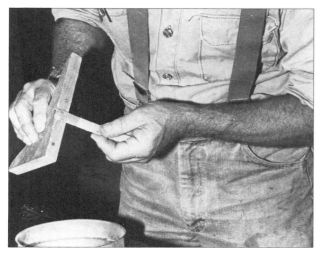

45 Then, apply epoxy to the knee's mating surfaces...

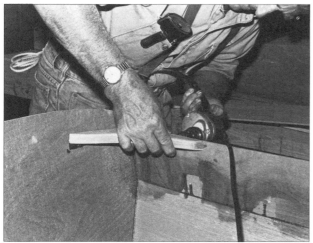

46 ...and screw it in place.

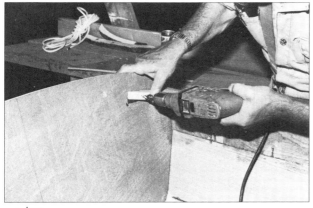

47 One 1" #8 screw (the farthest inboard) in each knee gets driven into the transom from inside. The other three quarter knees get fitted and attached just like this first one—flush with the top edge of the sheerstrake and angled up a little, as shown, at the transom.

THE GUARDRAILS

48 Draw a line along each sheerstrake's top, inner edge to serve as a drilling guide for the guardrail fastenings. The line should be located half the guardrail's width below the edge (1/2" for a standard 1" rail); at 6" intervals along this line, mark locations for the 3/4" #8 screws.

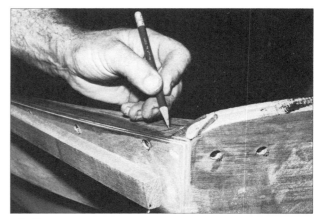

49 Mark where the screws you drove into the quarter knees are located, so you won't hit them with the guardrail fastenings.

50 Don't cut the guardrails to length until they have been fastened in place; you'll find the extra length useful in installing them. Clamp the guardrails, one at a time, to the boat, about 1/8" below the sheerstrake's top edge. (Both sheerstrake and guardrail will be planed down together, along with the quarter knees, later on.) Drill from the outside at the bow and stern, where you can drive 1–1/4" #8 screws into the knees.

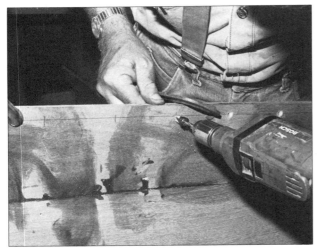

51 Elsewhere, the screws are driven from the inside and are located in accordance with the guidelines marked earlier. Guardrails are to be epoxied as well as screwed into place.

52 Now is a good time to dress down the tops of the transoms as well as the sheer. The drawing shows what the finished shape should be. A plane...

53 ...spokeshave...

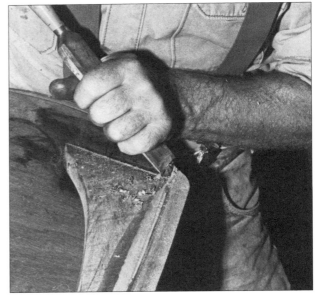

54 ...and chisel are the proper tools, followed by sandpaper.

THE SEATS

55 The seats should now be positioned according to the drawing; the after one is spaced 3" forward of the transom, to allow storage space for the rudder and daggerboard. Note from the drawing that the seat edges are to be chamfered on their lower corners for a more delicate appearance.

56 When the seat is the same distance down from the plank lap on each side of the boat, and fits the hull where shown on the drawing, a line marked on the hull underneath it will locate the top of the seat support block.

57 The seat support blocks are to be cut to length from the single long piece of stock furnished. Round the two inboard corners of each block for a finished appearance; a little trimming will be needed on the back side of each one before it will fit the slightly curved surface of the planking. With this accomplished, holes can be drilled (from the inside to establish location, then from the outside for the 1" #8 screws themselves).

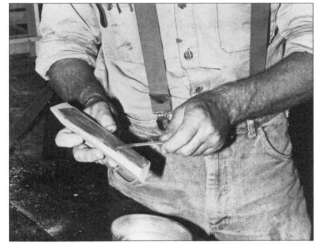

58 A bit of epoxy, and the block is ready to be permanently attached. There is a block under each end of each seat, and all are to be similarly installed, followed by the seats themselves. The seats, however, are fastened only with screws (2" #14) so they can be removed, when necessary, for painting. You'll probably do best now, in fact, to fit and drill the seats, and put off fastening them in until all the painting is completed.

59 A sculling notch centered in the top of the transom is handy for more than just sculling. It retains the oar you might decide to steer with, and it can also be used to guide the rode of an anchor you may someday wish to set from a larger boat. Cut the notch out to the size shown on the drawing, and round off its corners with a rasp and sandpaper.

THE DAGGERBOARD TRUNK

If you are building the sailing version, now is the time to install the daggerboard trunk, starting with Step 60; if you are building the rowing version, skip ahead to Step 91 and start installing the outer keel.

60 Start construction by attaching the 3/8" trunk sides to their rabbeted bedlogs, first drilling for the 3/4" #8 screws...

61 ...then applying epoxy to the mating surfaces...

62 ...and screwing the pieces together.

63 If the side and the bedlog don't come quite flush, plane as necessary for a smooth surface so the endposts will fit well. When one side assembly is finished, go on and build the other.

64 This is the way the trunk goes together—two side assemblies with a post at each end.

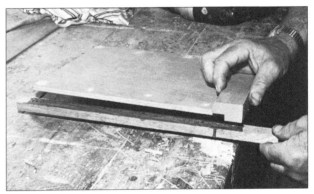

65 Select one side assembly and fasten it to the posts, drilling the screw holes before spreading the epoxy, as usual...

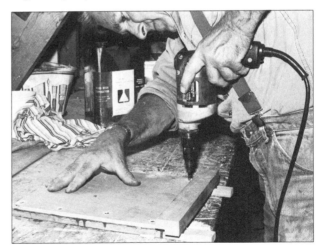

66 ...then driving the fastenings. Make sure that the posts are placed flush with the edges of the side pieces and that they project about an inch below the bedlogs. These projections will, once the trunk is installed, penetrate the boat's bottom to align the trunk over its slot and help in forming a watertight joint.

67 Now turn over the assembly you've just made and set the second side in place so that both bedlog bases are aligned.

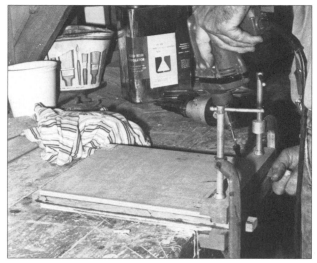

68 Clamp to hold this alignment and drill for the fastenings, just as you did for the first side, but with holes staggered so the screws from one side don't interfere with those from the other.

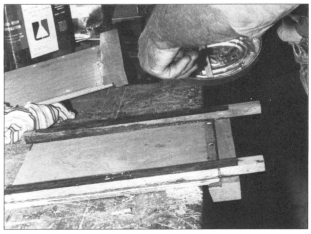

69 As always after drilling, clean the surfaces, spread the epoxy...

70 ...and screw the final side in place.

71 Be sure to clean off the excess epoxy. On the inside of the trunk, a rag on a stick helps with the cleanup.

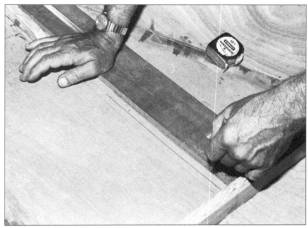

72 Cut back the projecting ends of both posts to half their width, and round them as shown on the drawings. The distance between them (as cut and rounded) establishes the length of the slot you'll be cutting in the boat's bottom; you can measure for slot length as shown, or better yet, mark the ends of the slot directly by holding the trunk in position against the 'midship frame and tracing around the posts.

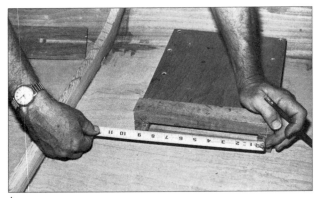

73 As shown on the drawing, the daggerboard's 9/16"-wide slot is located off-center to starboard so that it clears the boat's outer keel by about 1/8". (If you are adding a daggerboard trunk to an already-built rowing model whose outer keel is in place, you should increase the trunk's off-center distance to about 2" so that the inboard bedlog can be fastened up through the bottom, clear of the keel.) Mark the slot outline for cutting with a straightedge.

74 The 9/16"-diameter holes at the ends of the slot are made by boring downward until the spur of the bit (but not its flutes) comes through and shows underneath. Don't let your bit cut all the way through, or you may break off large splinters from the bottom.

75 Using the pilot holes thus made as locators, bore up through from under the boat to make a clean, full-sized hole, as shown here.

76 Cut along the lines between the holes with a sabersaw.

77 Then smooth the edges to a uniform 9/16" width with a wood rasp.

78 Now for the fitting of trunk to slot. The projecting ends of the posts should fit tightly in the slot, and the bedlogs should be scribed for a tight fit. (Scribing means marking a line all around the trunk that is a constant distance up from the boat's bottom; use a pencil compass, or a little block of wood as a shim under the pencil, for a scribing tool.) Make sure the unit stands plumb while you're fitting it; a combination square, shown here, helps establish vertical alignment.

79 Remove the trunk after scribing it, clamp it in a vise as shown, and plane down its underside to the scribeline. Use either a rabbet plane (shown) or a spokeshave for this purpose.

80 You'll need a chisel, rather than a plane, to cut away the end-grain of the posts.

81 After proving the trunk's fit in the boat, mark around its base, remove it for access, and drill holes out through the hull as shown, to locate the larger holes (for the 1–1/2" #10 screws) that are to be drilled from the outside. Put the trunk back in position and hold it there for this outside drilling, so that the holes go into the bedlogs as well as through the boat's bottom.

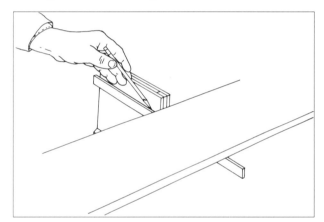

82 Now, before the trunk is permanently installed, is a good time to mark and cut its top to the correct height and angle. Lay the 'midship seat temporarily in place on its support blocks, just aft of the 'midship frame, so the seat's forward edge nearly touches the trunk. Mark the trunk on one of its sides by means of a straightedge held tight under the seat and lapping past the trunk. This establishes the cutting angle, but not the height. Now remove the trunk and lay the seat in its correct fore-and-aft position (notches in seat engaging 'midship frame), and measure how high its forward edge is off the boat's bottom. Add 1/4" and transfer this to the trunk, measuring upward along the trunk's aft end.

All drawings by Kathy Bray

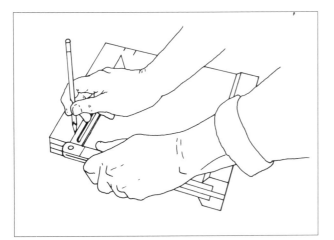

83 Use a bevel gauge to transfer the angle-of-cut line to the mark just made, then saw off the trunk to this height and plane it smooth.

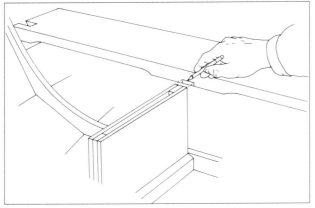

84 Set the trunk back in position in the boat, make sure it is plumb, and use it to mark the seat itself for the notch that is to be cut in its underside. Cut the notch and check that the fit is OK.

85 Now (finally!) the trunk can be permanently installed. Slather adhesive bedding compound, such as polysulfide or polyurethane, on the bottom of the boat, against the 'midship frame...

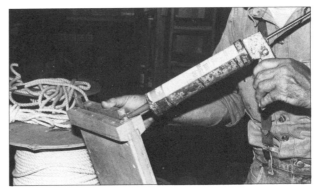

86 ...and on the underside of the trunk itself; then...

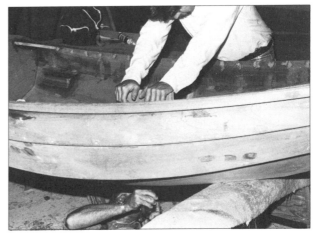

87 ...get your spouse, child, or a friend to press the unit firmly into place while you drive the screws up from below to hold it that way.

88 And, as always, scrape up the squeezed-out bedding compound.

THE DAGGERBOARD & TRUNK CAP

89 Now that you've got a trunk, you'll need a daggerboard to go in it and keep the boat from sliding off sideways when you're trying to sail ahead. (The daggerboard and trunk cap can be built at any time, since these pieces are separate from the hull. If you want to put them off for now, skip to Step 91 and install the outer keel.) Daggerboard assembly is simple: taper the edges that will be exposed to passing water as shown on the plan and in this picture; then attach the retainer cheeks at the top (mark their position by inserting the daggerboard in the trunk and tracing along the trunk's top edge). Attach the cheeks with epoxy only; you don't need screws. Cheeks are to be sawn flush with the aft edge of the daggerboard so they won't interfere with the 'midship seat. Paint should match the boat's interior, since the daggerboard will spend most of its time stored in view behind the aft seat.

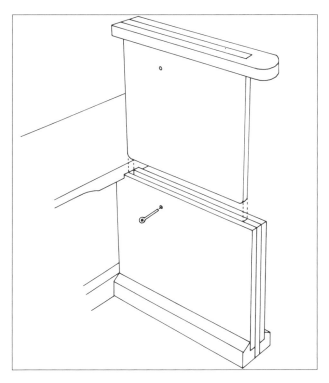

90 Make the trunk cap at the same time that you make the daggerboard, since the construction is similar. Experience has shown that there is a definite need for this kind of cap. Its tongue keeps the cap itself in place and occupies enough of the slot to keep water from pouring in when the pram is towed at high speed. Always use the cap—gasketed and pinned in place, if you want extra security. No one should have to deal with a full-of-water tender on the end of a towline.

THE KEEL

91 Taper the outer keel (in cross-section) as shown on the drawing by marking guidelines 1/16" in from each bottom corner and planing away the wood outside these lines. This is an optional, but desirable, operation which will make your boat look better; it will have little, if any, effect on performance.

92 Turn the boat upside down and saw off the projecting ends of the daggerboard trunk posts; then clean off any excess adhesive/bedding compound that would interfere with installing the outer keel. Mark two parallel lines 3/4" apart, straddling the boat's fore-and-aft centerline; these will locate the keel and be clear of the daggerboard's slot by about 1/8".

93 Drill locator holes at 6" intervals between the guidelines as shown. Holes for the 1" #8 screws themselves should be bored back up through the locator holes while the keel is temporarily held in position (by another person) between the marked guidelines. (If there is a slight warp or twist in the keel as furnished, don't be concerned. Simply straighten it by keeping it within the guidelines as you bore the fastening holes.)

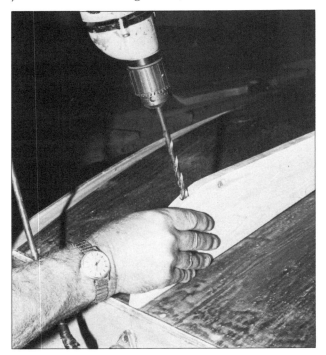

94 There will be one countersunk machine screw (1/4" x 4") in the aft end of the keel to strengthen it and pull it snugly into the hull. If you're shaky about boring this long hole freehand, set up some sighting sticks to keep the drill aligned.

95 Blow the surface clean of shavings, and spread adhesive bedding compound along the boat's bottom in between the marked guidelines.

96 Now, carefully lay the keel in place using the aft-end bolt, or one of the mid-length screws, to help locate it.

97 Get someone to help hold the keel while the screws are driven up from under the boat.

98 Drive the screws from the outside at the forward end in way of the forekeel—and sink them deep enough so that their heads won't interfere with the subsequent fairing or "nosing off." (Use a short batten, and mark a guideline for fairing now; it will show exactly how deep the screws have to be set.)

99 Drive and tighten the bolt at the keel's aft end.

100 Clean off the excess compound before it cures.

101 To resist wear from landing on the beach, the outer keel is shod for its full length with a chafing strip of 1/2" brass half-oval. To ready it for installation, the half-oval must be drilled (with a slight countersink to fit the screwheads) for the 1" #6 screws that will hold it in place. A drill press works best if you have one, although with more care, a hand-held drill can be used. Either way, be sure to centerpunch for the holes, about 6" apart (and offset from the outer keel fastenings) so the drill will start where it is supposed to.

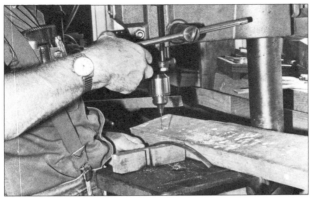

102 The chafing strip's aft end should first (before drilling) be bent to match the curve of the keel.

103 Complete drilling the screw holes (through the strip and into the keel) as you go along, starting at the aft end and working forward. Use the same bedding compound under it as for the outer keel.

104 Forward, to prepare a landing for the chafing strip, plane the keel's end (using the marks you made earlier as a guide) to form a fair transition around which the strip can be bent, and grind or file a 1/2"-wide "flat" along the seam between the two garboards over which the strip can lie. The photo shows what the area should look like.

105 If the forward end of the chafing strip sticks out beyond where it should, you can grind off the excess with a disc sander as shown, or simply use a hacksaw and file. The screw heads will also require filing to bring them flush with the chafing strip.

THE MASTSTEP

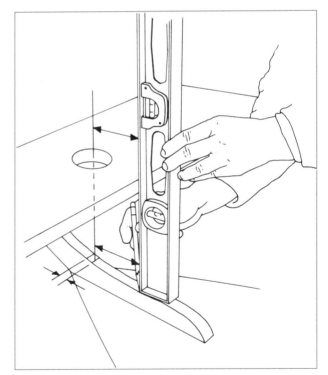

106 Fitting the maststep is one of the more sophisticated operations involved in building the NUTSHELL. The maststep has to notch over the forekeel and, at the same time, each of its ends has to fit against the hull planking. Besides that, the hole for the mast has to be centered athwartships and positioned 1/2" forward of the hole in the seat above (with the boat level) so that the mast will have the right amount of rake. If you carefully adhere to the following procedure, however, you should have no trouble.

Start by boring a 2–3/8"-diameter hole in the forward seat through which the mast can pass with a sliding fit. With the seat fastened in place and the boat leveled fore-and-aft according to the drawing, plumb down to the forekeel from the aft edge of the seat and make a reference mark. Measure forward from this mark a distance equal to that from seat edge to hole center plus 1/2", and make another mark. This is where the maststep (and, ultimately, the hole bored through it) should center.

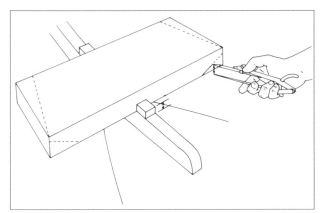

107&108 Now set the maststep in the boat so that the slot in its underside lies directly above the forekeel, and so that the step itself is in the correct fore-and-aft location above the mark made in the previous step. Naturally, the uncut step will be considerably too high at this stage—and you need to know exactly *how much* too high in order to scribe it for a proper fit. Determine this amount to be cut by making a 3/4"-wide shim to fill the gap between the top of the fore- keel and the underside of the maststep's slot; the height of this shim is the amount that the step has to be lowered in order to fit.

Set a pencil compass to the same height as the shim, and, holding it vertically with its metal point against the hull, mark the forward and aft edges of the step for a fit at each side of the boat. Remove the step, connect these marked lines across the other two faces of the step with a straightedge (or, alternatively, scribe the precise top-surface curve directly from the boat with the step in place). Cut to your marked lines, check for fit and mark the high spots, and plane down these beveled ends of the step until you have achieved a good fit.

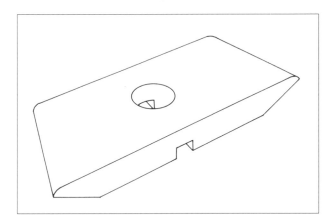

109 Fastening procedure is the same as for the daggerboard installation: mark inside, bore out, bore in, clean, bed, and fasten. But first, bore the tapered hole for the heel of the mast—at an angle (because of the mast rake and the step's incline), which you can lift off the drawing or the boat itself with a bevel gauge.

THE RUDDER AND TILLER

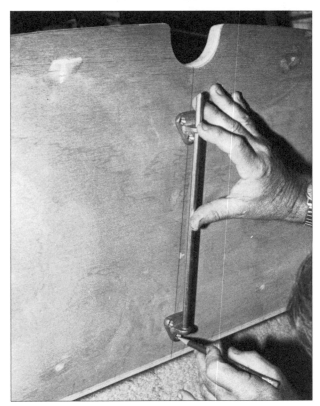

110 The rudder hangs on the transom of the pram, supported by a vertical rod with flange mounts. Mark a vertical centerline on the transom face, if you haven't done so earlier, and use it for sideways alignment. The up-and-down position is as shown on the drawing. When the unit is where you want it, bore right through the transom for the 1–1/4" #10 flathead machine screws that will hold it there.

111 Spread the flanges with bedding compound before final installation.

112 Attachment to the transom is made with three machine screws through each mounting flange. Projecting ends of the screws are to be hacksawn flush with their nuts after tightening.

113 The rudder is not much more complicated than the daggerboard. First, smooth the curved edge of the cheek pieces that will lie along the flat of the blade and would be hard to smooth up after assembly. Don't bother with the cheeks' other edges at this point, since they can be more easily and accurately dressed down after the cheeks have been epoxied to the blade.

114 Next, glue the cheeks to the rudder blade, one on each side. Hold position and apply pressure with clamps as shown while the epoxy sets up. After the epoxy cures, plane the rudder assembly's edges to shape and rivet the two bronze gudgeons in place as shown on the plan. (The open gudgeon which goes at the bottom will have to be cut to length.)

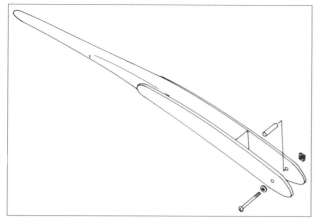

115 The tiller goes together in the same manner as the rudder does, with cheek pieces on each side, and you can be as creative as you wish in shaping it. Just make sure the distance between the cheeks matches the thickness of the rudderhead, and that the tiller's bushing/machine screw location gets transferred to the rudder for use in shaping the notch in its aft edge. All this shows on the drawings, and you should have no trouble if you keep referring to them.

OTHER DETAILS

116 At this stage, you should fill over all the screw heads and face up other holes or imperfections, then give the hull a thorough sanding inside and out. (If you're building the sailing version, do the same for the rudder, daggerboard, spars, and tiller.) The objective, of course, is to produce a smooth, fair surface for painting or varnishing. Pay particular attention to removing the dried, overspread epoxy.

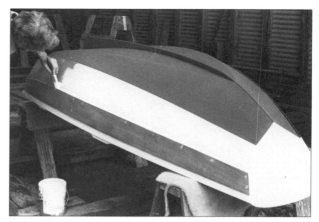

117 Before painting, bore a hole through the bow transom, just above the top of the forekeel, for the rope painter (towline) that the boat will be tied up with. The oarlock plates can be installed now or after painting; they simply fasten to the inside of the hull, as shown on the drawing, with #10–32 machine screws (nuts inboard) in way of the guardrail. There are limitless combinations of colors that, along with stripes and other painted decoration, will look good on your pram. Have fun with her color scheme; you can always change it.

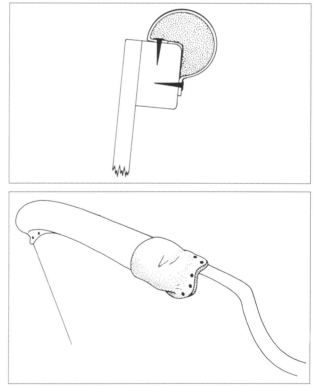

118 Oars can either be purchased or made from scratch. We recommend flat-bladed oars about 6–1/2' long. If you'll be using your NUTSHELL as a tender for another boat, she will need some kind of soft fender material all around her rails and around at least part of the transom–top. Canvas-covered rubber, molded commercially to a 3/4–round shape, makes a neat–looking job, and the cut ends can be capped with a piece of leather, tacked in place. We've found it best to staple or copper–tack its upper flange to the top of the guardrail first—from the inside out, so that the upper flange is hidden when the fender is pulled down into position for fastening its lower flange. This flange can then be fastened to the outboard face of the wooden guardrail near the rail's lower corner. If you use staples, make sure they're bronze or Monel, so that they won't rust.

119 The spars furnished with your sailing kit have been tapered and made 8-sided, so they require only some finish planing and sanding to make them round and smooth. There is some additional shaping needed at the end of each spar, but it is straightforward work and shows clearly on the drawings. The spars can be oiled, varnished, or painted when they're complete—or they can even be left bare.

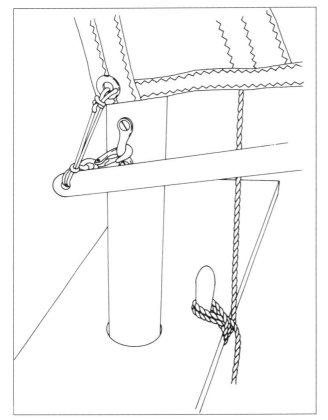

120 The lathe-turned, wooden belaying pin stuck through a hole in the forward seat as shown on the drawings makes an elegant halyard belay; there are other effective methods, however, for holding up the sail.

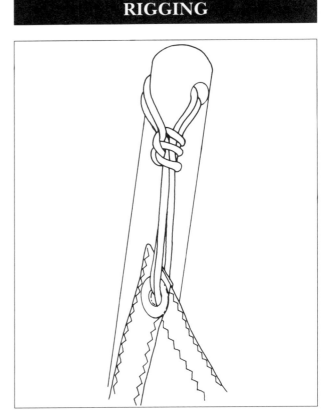

121 Rigging your NUTSHELL is simple. First, using light, braided nylon line, lash the head of the sail to the yard by putting a seizing at each corner and a spiral lacing through the sail's grommet eyes and around the yard, working from one end to the other. (Each seizing should begin with a bowline tied in the sail's corner eye, passed through the hole in the yard, and back through the sail's eye. Make two or three passes in this manner.) Then, with about 8' of the line, spiral along the yard itself, out to the peak, through the hole in the yard, and back through the sail's eye a couple of times; then knot the hauling part to part of the seizing you have just made. The idea here is to pull the sail out *along* the yard with the first passes (the ones through the hole in the yard), then hold it *against* the yard with the final turns.

122 The boom is loose-footed, held to the sail only at the ends where a seizing like that described above should be made. You'll also need to seize a snaphook at the boom's forward end for attaching it to the mast. (It snaps into a strapeye fastened to the mast's aft side, as shown on the drawing.)

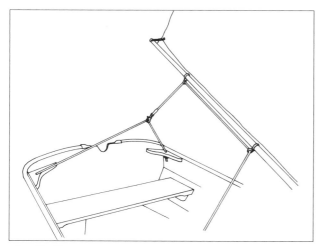

123 The sheet adjusts the sail's trim and is rigged to a rope traveler, which allows for better sail trim and better speed to windward. Bore a 5/16" hole in each of the quarter knees, insert one end of a 4' length of 1/4" Dacron line (which becomes the traveler) through one of the holes, and tie an overhand knot underneath; do the same with the other end, adjusting the second knot's location to give a little slack in the span between the knees. The sheet itself consists of 16' of the same 1/4" Dacron line as that used for the traveler. A snaphook should be spliced into one of its ends (this will ride on the rope traveler), and the other end should be whipped so it won't unlay. We've found that a couple of sailmakers' small brass thimbles, seized to the boom—one above the traveler, and one about 3' ahead of it—work well as sheet fairleads.

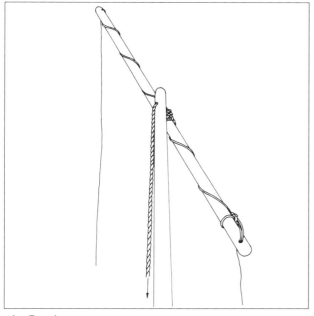

124 The halyard—18' of the same 1/4" Dacron line—ties to the yard, where the drawing shows, with a clove hitch (finished with an overhand knot overtop to hold it). It reeves up through the hole in the masthead, and comes down to the belaying pin in the forward seat. Both the halyard's ends should be whipped to avoid fraying.

125 There's nothing tricky about sailing the NUTSHELL, just a few things to keep in mind that will enhance its performance:

A) Sit on the bottom, or kneel just aft of the middle seat; a person's weight on the aft seat gets the boat out of trim and makes tacking awkward. Keep the boat in level fore-and-aft trim.

B) Keep the halyard tight, and fine-tune the sail's set by moving the halyard's attachment to the yard. (An inch or two one way or the other makes a noticeable difference in how the sail sets.) You should strive to keep the sail smooth, without diagonal wrinkles caused by a slack leech.

C) Close-hauled sail trim should bring the boom over the lee corner of the transom; further trimming, although tempting, will improve your heading but drastically reduce your speed.

D) Hold the sheet; don't belay it. Being able to instantly let it go in a puff will avoid a capsize.

E) It is always essential to know how and when to shorten sail, and you should never venture off without having familiarized yourself and your crew with the steps involved. Installing a row of reefpoints in the sail would be a prudent step, but in a pinch, you could lash the yard to the mast so as to create a triangular sail of very reduced area. *In any case, use caution as the wind increases; it is a very powerful force!*

F) Like any unballasted wooden boat, the NUTSHELL pram will float awash when filled with water. But in the event of a capsize in deep water, it is not easy to get the water out! First, the water tends to wash over the sides when conditions are choppy; second, it may come up through the daggerboard trunk, unless the board or the cap can be secured in place. In order to lighten the load of bailing a swamped pram, and thus to further ensure the safety of the crew, we recommend installing flotation to increase the positive buoyancy of the wood hull. Styrofoam adhered to the undersides of the seats, or inflatable rollers placed under the seats, will add considerably to the buoyancy.

ADDITIONAL NOTES ON GETTING STARTED
WHEN YOU'RE BUILDING FROM SCRATCH

Pulling together all the materials is, of course, the first step in any building job, and the Nutshell is no exception. A list of what you'll need is included on the drawings. The second step is to cut out the bow and stern transoms and to glue up and shape the 'midship frame and the fore keel. These pieces, together with the two temporary molds, will soon be set up and held in position on a jig to form the skeleton around which the hull is planked.

CUTTING OUT THE TRANSOMS

Making the bow and stern transoms is simply a matter of carefully cutting them out of sheet plywood to the shapes shown on the plan. Note that their edges are beveled for the planking that will lay against them. These bevels are shown on the plan in degrees referenced from the *small* face of each transom. (Make sure you have squared this away in your mind before you do any cutting; otherwise, you're likely to have transoms that are too small for the boat.)

MAKING THE FORE KEEL AND 'MIDSHIP FRAME

Now for the laminates. Both the 'midship frame and the fore keel have to be bent over and clamped to forms representing their inside curves and held there until the glue dries. A full-sized pattern of each piece, laid out from the dimensions given on the drawing, will establish the curve of the bending form as well as give you the final trim size of the laminates. The forms can be built of any inch-thick scrap lumber; the photo shows one way of building the form for the 'midship frame.

The $1/8$"-thick by 1"-wide fir strips that make up the laminates should be sawn out so as to make a stack slightly thicker than what you'll eventually need, say about $2^3/8$" for the fore keel and $2^1/8$" for the frame. Spread glue on both mating surfaces of each strip, and place them all in position, using waxed paper or sheet plastic to keep them from sticking to the form or the floor; then clamp them securely to the form, as shown in the photo for the 'midship frame. The fore keel is handled in the same way.

After the glue dries and the pieces are removed from their bending forms, you should dress off their faces so that they are smooth and the finished thickness is about $3/4$". Use a thickness planer or power plane if you have them; otherwise, a scraper and hand plane will do. You can then lay on your patterns with the inner curves aligned, mark around them, saw and plane to the lines, and the pieces will be almost ready for setting up.

Before that comes the important task of carefully marking the reference lines: the vertical centerline and sheerline of the frame, the No. 1 station line on the fore keel. And if you haven't yet put the center- and sheerlines on the transom faces, now's the time for that. After marking all the pieces, you can install the temporary cross spall on the 'midship frame, as shown in the plan. Now you're all set to move on to building the molds and jig.